Portrait of a Marriage

Nigel Nicolson

A Phoenix Paperback

Portrait of a Marriage by Nigel Nicolson
first published in Great Britain
by Weidenfeld & Nicolson Limited in 1973

This abridged edition published in 1996 by Phoenix
a division of Orion Books Ltd
Orion House, 5 Upper St Martin's Lane, London WC2H 9EA

1 85799 567 8

Typeset at The Spartan Press Ltd
Lymington, Hants
Printed in Great Britain by
Clays Ltd, St Ives plc

Foreword by Nigel Nicolson

When my mother, Vita Sackville-West, died in 1962, it was my duty as her executor to go through her personal papers. She was careful about such things, and had filed everything of importance, including all her letters to and from Harold Nicolson during the fifty years of their engagement and marriage, and all her own diaries and the diaries of her mother, Lady Sackville. In the forty pinewood drawers of a large Italian cupboard I found hundreds of letters from the friends who had meant most to her since her childhood. At the time I read very little, making a mental note that while all the material existed for a full record of her life, it should be allowed to simmer.

I took a final look round her sitting-room in the tower at Sissinghurst (a room which I had entered only half a dozen times in the previous thirty years), and came upon a locked Gladstone bag lying in the corner of the little turret-room which opens off it. The bag contained something – a tiara in its case, for all I knew. Having no key, I cut the leather from around its lock to open it. Inside was a large notebook in a flexible cover, page after page filled by her neat pencilled manuscript. I carried it to her writing-table and began to read. The first few pages were abortive drafts of a couple of short stories. The sixth page was headed '23 July 1920', followed by a narrative in the first person which continued for eighty more. I read it through to the end without stirring from her table. It was an auto-biography written when she was aged twenty-eight, a confession, an attempt to purge her mind and heart of a love which had possessed her, a love for another woman, Violet Trefusis.

The simplicity of it, its candour, the extraordinary sequence of events which it unfolded, her implicit plea for forgiveness and compassion, for the strength to resist further temptation, stirred me deeply. I had long known the barest outlines of the story (but not from her) and here was every detail of it, written with scarcely an erasure or correction at a moment when the wound was still fresh and painful. Although her narrative began uncertainly with a rambling account of her childhood, when she came to the heart of her problem it grew in power and intensity, sharpened by a novelist's instinctive variation of mood and speed, almost as if it were not her own experience that she was describing but another's.

It is the story of two people who married for love and whose love deepened with every passing year, although each was constantly and by mutual consent unfaithful to the other. Both loved people of their own sex, but not exclusively. Their marriage not only survived infidelity, sexual incompatibility and long absences, but became stronger and finer as a result. Each came to give the other full liberty without enquiry or reproach. Honour was rooted in dishonour. Their marriage succeeded because each found permanent and undiluted happiness only in the company of the other. If their marriage is seen as a harbour, their love-affairs were mere ports-of-call. It was to the harbour that each returned; it was there that both were based.

This book is therefore a panegyric of marriage, although it describes a marriage which was superficially a failure because it was incomplete. They achieved their ideal companionship only after a long struggle which was still not ended when Vita Sackville-West wrote the last words of her confession, but once achieved it was unalterable and life-long, and they made of it (as I wrote in the Introduction to my father's Diaries, without revealing the extent of their difficulties) one of the strangest and most successful unions that two gifted people have ever enjoyed.

Of course I have no right whatsoever to write down the truth about my life, involving as it naturally does the lives of so many other people, but I do so urged by a necessity of truthtelling, because there is no living soul who knows the complete truth; here, may be one who knows a section; and there, one who knows another section: but to the whole picture not one is initiated. Having written it down I shall be able to trust no one to read it; there is only one person in whom I have such utter confidence that I would give every line of this confession into his hands, knowing that after wading through this morass — for it is a morass, my life, a bog, a swamp, a deceitful country, with one bright patch in the middle, the patch that is unalterably his — I know that after wading through it all he would emerge holding his estimate of me steadfast. This would be the test of my confidence, from which I would not shrink. I would not give it to *her* — perilous touchstone!, who even in these first score of lines should teach me where truth lies. I *do* know where it lies, but have no strength to grasp it; here am I already in the middle of my infirmities.

I realize that this confession, autobiography, whatever I may call it, must necessarily have for its outstanding fault a lack of all proportion. I have got to trust to a very uncertain memory, and whereas the present bulks enormous, the past is misty. I can't remember much about my childhood, except that I had very long legs and very straight hair, over which Mother used to hurt my feelings and say she couldn't bear to look at me because I was so ugly. I know that I wasn't a physical coward in those days, because I can remember doing dangerous things on a bicycle and climbing high trees – and yet, stop, I do believe I must have been a coward already, because I can remember thinking a great deal about whether I should be brave the next day when I went out riding, and I was too much fascinated by seeing other people do things which I knew I shouldn't dare to do myself. I never realized this until this moment. Anyway, I wasn't so much of a coward, and I kept my nerves under control, and made a great ideal of being hardy, and as like a boy as possible. I know I was cruel to other children, because I remember stuffing their nostrils with putty and beating a little boy with stinging-nettles, and I lost nearly all my friends in that kind of way, until none of the local children would come to tea with me except those who had acted as my allies and lieutenants.

I don't remember much more about myself as a child than that. I remember more about outside things. I don't remember either my father or mother very vividly at that time, except that Dada used to take me for terribly long walks and talk to me about science, principally Darwin, and I liked him a great deal better than Mother, of whose quick temper I was frightened. I don't even remember thinking her pretty, which she must have been – lovely, even. My impression of her was that I couldn't be rough when she was there, or naughty, and so it was really a great relief when she went away. I remember very vividly terrible scenes between her and Dada – at least, she made the scene, he usually said nothing at all, or very mildly, 'Oh, come, dear, is that quite accurate?' Her statements rarely *were* accurate; I realized this, very, very slowly, but was incredibly obtuse over it; in fact I didn't really grasp it until a comparatively short time ago. (Evening is coming on, and I shall soon have to stop writing; thank God I am alone tonight.)

When I was about twelve I started to write. (It was *Cyrano de Bergerac* that first initiated me to the possibilities of literature!) I never stopped writing after that – historical novels, pretentious, quite uninteresting, pedantic, and all written at unflagging speed: the day after one was finished another would be begun. I think that between the ages of thirteen and nineteen I must have been quite dreadful. I was plain, priggish, studious (oh, very!), totally uninspired, unmanageably and lankily tall, in fact the only good thing that could be said of me was that I wouldn't have anything to do with my kind. Seeing that I was unpopular (and small wonder, for a saturnine prig), I wouldn't court popularity. I minded rather, and used to

3

cry when I went to bed after coming home from a party, but I made myself defiant about it. I don't mean this to sound in the least pathetic; I wasn't unhappy, only solitary, but I don't pretend that I minded solitude, I rather chose it. (Looking back, I think I maligned myself rather by calling myself totally uninspired: I had flaring days, oh yes, I did!, when I thought I was going to electrify the world; it was like being drunk, and I can find traces of it now in the margins of all those ponderous, interminable books I wrote – two little letters, V.E., which stood for 'very easy', and I look at them now, and re-read the leaden stuff which they are supposed to qualify, and take upon trust that I found those now forgotten moments full of splendour.)

These years are tedious to write about – tedious, and very uncertain. I mean the years from thirteen to nineteen. Things happened, of course, things that made an impression and changed me – not that I changed much, or grew any more sophisticated. What happened? Let me try to remember: there is writing, always writing, and moroseness, and periods of real hard work and proficiency at the daily school to which I went every autumn and winter term in London. I set myself to triumph at that school, and I did triumph – I beat everybody there, sooner or later, and at the end-of-term exams I thought I had done badly if I didn't carry off at least six out of eight first prizes. I think I was quite self-conscious over this: if I couldn't be popular, I would be clever; and I did succeed in getting a reputation of being clever, which was quite unmerited, for I am distinctly *not* clever, but which like all reputations has died hard. I don't believe it is quite dead yet – people say, 'Oh yes, she writes doesn't she?', implying that one must be clever in order to write. I wasn't hated at that school, at least I don't think so; I think they quite liked me. But I really cared not a scrap whether they liked me or not. Those were my most savage years! I worked very hard, and became more pedantic than ever. I've got a scholarly turn of mind, let me face that damning truth.

Other things happened too. I acquired a friend – I, who was the worst person in the world at making friends, closed instantaneously in friendship, or almost instantaneously (to be exact, the second time we saw each other), with Violet [Keppel, later Trefusis]. I was thirteen, she was two years younger, but in every instinct she might have been six years my senior. It seems to me so significant now that I should remember with such distinctness my first sight of her; we met at a tea-party by the bedside of a mutual friend with a broken leg, and she made to me some little remark about the flowers in the room. I wasn't listening; and so didn't answer. This piqued her – she was already spoilt. She got her mother to ask mine to send me to tea. I went. We sat in a darkened room, and talked – about our ancestors, of all strange topics – and in the hall as I left she kissed me. I made up a little song that evening, 'I've got a friend!'. I remember so well. I sang it in my bath.

I long to stop over Violet – to tell how much I secretly admired her, and how proud I was of the friendship of this

5

brilliant, this extraordinary, this almost unearthly creature, but how I treated her with unvarying scorn, my one piece of really able handling; which kept her to me as no proof of devotion would have kept her – but I am going to tell other things first, because all the present is filled with Violet, and during the past she appears constantly too. I will stop only to say that from the beginning I was utterly sure of her; she might be elusive, she might be baffling, she might even be faithless, but under everything I had the rather insolent (but justified) certainty of her keeping to me. I listened to stories about her with a superior and proprietary smile. I would have remained for ten years without hearing a word from her, and at the end of those ten years I would have held the same undamaged confidence that we must inevitably re-unite. There isn't a word of exaggeration in these statements – nothing, for that matter, in the whole of this writing is to be exaggerated or 'arranged'; its only merit will be truth, but truth as bleak as I can make it.

It was just then, however, that I first met Harold. He arrived late at a small dinner-party before a play, very young and alive and charming, and the first remark I ever heard him make was, 'What fun', when he was asked by his hostess to act as host. Everything was fun to his energy, vitality, and buoyancy. I liked his irrepressible brown curls, his laughing eyes, his charming smile, and his boyishness. But we didn't become particular friends. I think he looked on me as more of a child than I actually was, and as for myself I never thought about people, especially men, under a very personal aspect unless they made quite definite friendly advances to me first; even then I think one wonders sometimes what people are driving at.

I was eighteen then and he was twenty-three.

That summer [1910] I caught a heaven-sent attack of pneumonia, and as a consequence of my being ordered abroad we spent the whole winter from November till April in the South of France near Monte Carlo.

Harold meanwhile was in Madrid, and, but for an interlude when I dragged a plaintive but self-sacrificing Mother to Florence in the spring, the rest of the year was a repetition of the experience of being 'out'. But now something else happens – something which, I would like to emphasize, started in complete innocence on my part. I want to be frank. I have implied, I think, that men didn't attract me, that I didn't think of them in what is called 'that way'. Women did. Rosamund did. Rosamund [Grosvenor] was the neat little girl who came to play with me when Dada went to South Africa. She had come out to stay at Monte Carlo – invited by Mother, not by me; I would never have dreamt of asking anyone to stay with me; even Violet had never spent more than a week at Knole: I resented invasion. Still, as Rosamund came, once she was there, I naturally spent most of the day with her, and after I had got back to England, I suppose it was resumed. I don't remember very clearly, but the fact remains that by the middle of that summer we were inseparable, and moreover were living on terms of the greatest possible intimacy. But I want to say again that the thing did start in comparative innocence. Oh, I dare say I realized vaguely that I had no business to sleep with Rosamund, and I should certainly never have allowed anyone to find out, but my sense of guilt went no further than that.

Anyway I was very much in love with Rosamund.

Harold came back from Madrid at the end of that summer [1911]. He had been very ill out there, and I remember him as rather a pathetic figure wrapped up in an Ulster on a warm summer day, who was able to walk slowly round the garden with me. All that time while I was 'out' is extremely dim to me, very largely I think, owing to the fact that I was living a kind of false life that left no impression upon me. Even my liaison with Rosamund was, in a sense, superficial. I meant that it was almost exclusively physical, as, to be frank, she always bored me as a companion. I was very fond of her, however; she had a sweet nature. But she was quite stupid.

Harold wasn't. He was as gay and clever as ever, and I loved his brain and his youth, and was flattered at his liking for me. He came to Knole a good deal that autumn and winter, and people began to tell me he was in love with me, which I didn't believe was true, but wished that I could believe it. I wasn't in love with him then – there was Rosamund – but I did like him better than anyone, as a companion and playfellow, and for his brain and his delicious disposition. I hoped that he would propose to me before he went away to Constantinople, but felt diffident and sceptical about it.

He had never even made love to me – not by a single word – and I only knew he liked me because he always tried to be with me, and wrote to me whenever he had to go away. Besides, people had put it into my head. I had always thought they were wrong, but they weren't, and that night at the [Hatfield] ball he asked me to marry him, and I said I would. He was very shy, and pulled all the buttons one by one off his gloves; and I was frightened, and tried to prevent him from coming to the point.

He didn't kiss me, but we sat rather bewildered over supper afterwards, and talked excitedly though vaguely about the flat we would have in Rome. I had on a new dress.

Only two or three days remained before he had to go away to Constantinople. I went up to London next day and told Mother I was engaged to him, but we were forbidden to write to one another except as ordinary friends, because we were too young, and also there was the question of money. We spent those two or three days together at Knole, and my impression is that we walked the whole time at a great speed through wet grass. Then he went away, and I got ill and was very depressed and miserable. Mother used to come to my room once or twice a day holding a little green bottle of disinfectant to her nose, and saying that there were three hundred steps between her room and mine, and what a bore it was feeling one had to go and see someone who was ill and waiting for one, so that after she had gone away again I used to sob with depression.

When I got better I also got more cheerful, and the Rosamund affair deepened. It was rather ironical that that affair should have started in the same house [The Grove, Watford] as where I spent the night of Harold's proposal. I went to Florence with her that spring, where, with an absurd old governess who had a mump on one side of her face and was always saying, 'Oh my dears, do consider your illustrious names', we shared a three-roomed cottage. I really was innocent over the Rosamund affair. It never struck me as wrong that I should be more or less engaged to Harold, and at the same time much in love with Rosamund. The fact is that I regarded Harold far more as a playfellow than in any other light. Our relationship was so fresh, so intellectual, so unphysical, that I never thought of him in that aspect at all. It was rather his own fault, after all, from the over-respectful way in which he had always treated me. I can best express what I mean about him by saying that he stood at the absolutely opposite pole from the lover-type of man. Some men seem to be born to be lovers, others to be husbands; he belongs to the latter category. Rosamund wasn't exactly jealous of him then; he was too far away, and our engagement was too vague, and she knew that although I was very fond of him I was passionately in love with herself – I use the word 'passionately' on purpose. It was passion that used to make my head swim sometimes, even in the daytime, but we never made love.

Harold came back on leave in August, and we spent most of the next two months together at Knole, but our engagement was still kept a secret and our behaviour was irreproachable. Rosamund was jealous of him then. I wish I could remember things better. One evening when we were out in the wet garden after a rainy day, he kissed me for the first time, and rather characteristically called me his wife. Looking back, I see how characteristic it is that he should always have thought of me in that way, but I must say I was thrilled then. After that we made a fuss and obtained that we might write to one another as though we were engaged. Rosamund minded dreadfully – as much from envy as from jealousy, I think. In October she, Harold and I, all three, went to Italy, travelling as far as Bologna together, and there Harold left us to go on to Constantinople by the Orient Express, while Rosamund and I went on to Florence.

I hate writing this, but I must, I must. When I began this I swore I would shirk nothing, and no more I will. So here is the truth: I was never so much in love with Rosamund as during those weeks in Italy and the months that followed. It may seem that I should have missed Harold more. I admit everything, to my shame, but I have never pretended to have anything other than a base and despicable character. I seem to be incapable of fidelity, as much then as now. But, as a sole justification, I separate my loves into two halves: Harold, who is unalterable, perennial, and *best*; there has never been anything but absolute purity in my love for Harold, just as there has never been anything but absolute purity in his nature. And on the other hand stands my perverted nature, which loved and tyrannized over Rosamund and ended by deserting her without one heart-pang, and which now is linked irremediably with Violet. I have here a scrap of paper on which Violet, intuitive psychologist, has scribbled, 'The upper half of your face is so pure and grave – almost childlike. And the lower half is so domineering, sensual, almost brutal – it is the most absurd contrast, and extraordinarily symbolical of your Dr Jekyll and Mr Hyde personality.' That is the whole crux of the matter, and I see now that my whole curse has been a duality with which I was too weak and too self-indulgent to struggle.

Things began to rush, after I came back from Spain. The delay over my engagement began to irritate me, and one day I wrote to Harold saying we had perhaps better give up the idea. He sent me a despairing telegram in reply, and then I scarcely know what happened inside my heart: something snapped, and I loved Harold from that day on; I think his energy in sending me a telegram impressed me, just as I was impressed when he came after me in an aeroplane when I ran away. Anyway, I wired back that everything was as before, and the letter which followed the telegram touched me greatly, for I saw by it how much he truly cared. But I continued my liaison with Rosamund. I say this with deep shame.

Violet was now back in England since a year, and I had seen her sometimes, but not very often, because Rosamund was even more jealous of her than of Harold and prevented me from going near her. So I really only saw her when she came to Knole for parties, but then I was always conscious of the same old undercurrent, and for that reason I never mentioned Harold to her; he was something separate. Once she came to my room in the middle of the night and asked me if I were in love; but that was sometime before, and I could say No quite truthfully. She always came like that when she had the chance, and she usually kissed me then – on my mouth, I mean – but we never did, even ordinarily, at other times. Violet was very amusing then and a terrible flirt, throwing over first one man and then another; she used to do all kinds of parlour-tricks, which I never saw, as she stopped immediately I came into the room, and if ever we met anywhere accidentally she would turn white to the lips. I used to amuse myself by taking her unaware in this way, and Dada in the innocence of his heart used to say, 'Did she turn pale?', as a joke.

Mother said we could be engaged and married in the autumn, so it was announced. Rosamund was miserable. She used to cry all night and every night, as I very well knew, because her bedroom was next door to mine at Knole, but as I had ceased to care for her and thought only of Harold, I was only exasperated by her tears and tried to stop them by getting angry, not by being sympathetic. I was cold as ice to her, and I see now what a beast I was, and how pathetic she was, because she really did adore me, and added to the misery of knowing that I cared for someone else, she must have felt that she had no one who cared two straws for her – except an obscure sailor whom she didn't like.

When we came back to Knole life became a jumble of letters, wedding-presents, and clothes, the whole being plentifully watered by Rosamund's tears. I have seldom seen anyone in such despair, but it didn't touch me. Mother lavished jewels on me. Harold and I grudged an hour spent away from one another. I hurry over this part, because it is the same for everybody. On the 1st of October [1913] we were married in the chapel at Knole, decked out like a theatre by me. Mother, who doesn't like being *émotionée*, stayed in bed. I had cried bitterly the evening before at the prospect of leaving Knole and giving up my liberty, but I had cried away all my regrets and had none left when the day came. Rosamund survived my wedding-day somehow, and rather splendidly rose to the occasion of hiding away her own sorrow; she is really rather splendid in some ways. Violet didn't come. I never told her anything about my engagement, and she learnt it through the papers and wrote me sarcastic letters through which I could read her anger.

That was my wedding.

In April [1918], when we were back in the country, Violet wrote to me to ask whether she could come and stay with me for a fortnight. I was bored by the idea, as I wanted to work, and I did not know how to entertain her; but I could scarcely refuse. So she came. We were both bored. My serenity got on her nerves, and her restlessness got on mine. She went up to London for the day as often as she could, but she came back in the evenings because the air-raids frightened her. She had been here [Long Barn] I think about a week when everything changed suddenly — changed far more than I foresaw at the time; changed my life. It was the 18th of April. An absurd circumstance gave rise to the whole thing; I had just got clothes like the women-on-the-land were wearing, and in the unac-customed freedom of breeches and gaiters I went into wild spirits; I ran, I shouted, I jumped, I climbed, I vaulted over gates, I felt like a schoolboy let out on a holiday; and Violet followed me across fields and woods with a new meekness, saying very little, but never taking her eyes off me, and in the midst of my exuberance I knew that all the old under-current had come back stronger than ever, and that my old domination over her had never been diminished. I remember that wild irresponsible day. It was one of the most vibrant days of my life. As it happened, Harold was not coming down that night. Violet and I dined alone together, and then after dinner, we went into my sitting-room, and for some time made conversation, but that broke down, and from ten o'clock until two in the morning – for four hours, or perhaps more – we talked.

Violet had struck the secret of my duality; she attacked me about it, and I made no attempt to conceal it from her or from myself. I talked myself out, until I could hear my own voice getting hoarse, and the fire went out, and all the servants had long since gone to bed, and there was not a soul in the house except Violet and me, and I talked out the whole of myself with absolute sincerity and pain, and Violet only listened – which was skilful of her. She made no comments and no suggestions until I had finished – until, that is, I had dug into every corner and brought its contents out to the light. I had been vouchsafed insight, as one sometimes is. Then, when I had finished, when I had told her how all the gentleness and all the femininity of me was called out by Harold alone, but how towards everyone else my attitude was completely otherwise – then, still with her infinite skill, she brought me round to my attitude towards herself, as it had always been ever since we were children, and then she told me how she had loved me always, and reminded me of incidents running through years, which I couldn't pretend to have forgotten. She was far more skilful than I. I might have been a boy of eighteen, and she a woman of thirty-five. She was infinitely clever – she didn't scare me, she didn't rush me, she didn't allow me to see where I was going; it was all conscious on her part, but on mine it was simply the drunkenness of liberation – the liberation of half my personality. She opened up to me a new sphere. And for her, of course, it meant the supreme effort to conquer the love of the person she had always wanted, who had always repulsed her (when things seemed to be going too far), out of a sort of fear, and of whom she was madly jealous – a fact I had not realized, so adept was she at concealment, and so obtuse was I at her psychology.

She lay on the sofa, I sat plunged in the armchair; she took my hands, and parted my fingers to count the points as she told me why she loved me. I hadn't dreamt of such an art of love. Such things had been *direct* for me always; I had known no love possessed of that Latin artistry (whether instinctive or acquired). I was infinitely troubled by the softness of her touch and the murmur of her lovely voice. She appealed to my unawakened senses; she wore, I remember, a dress of red velvet, that was exactly the colour of a red rose, and that made of her, with her white skin and the tawny hair, the most seductive being. She pulled me down until I kissed her – I had not done so for many years. Then she was wise enough to get up and go to bed; but I kissed her again in the dark after I had blown out our solitary lamp. She let herself go entirely limp and passive in my arms. (I shudder to think of the experience that lay behind her abandonment). I can't think I slept all that night – not that much of the night was left.

I don't know how to go on; I keep thinking that Harold, if he ever reads this, will suffer so, but I ask him to remember that he is reading about a *different person* from the one he knew. Also I am not writing this for fun, but for several reasons which I will explain. (1) As I started by saying, because I want to tell the *entire* truth. (2) Because I know of no truthful record of such a connection – one that is written, I mean, with no desire to appeal to a vicious taste in any possible readers; and (3) because I hold the conviction that as centuries go on, and the sexes become more nearly merged on account of their increasing resemblances, I hold the conviction that such connections will to a very large extent cease to be regarded as merely unnatural, and will be understood far better, at least in their *intellectual* if not in their physical aspect. (Such is already the case in Russia.) I believe that then the psychology of people like myself will be a matter of interest, and I believe it will be recognized that many more people of my type do exist than under the present-day system of hypocrisy is commonly admitted. I am not saying that such personalities, and the connections which result from them, will not be deplored as they are now; but I do believe that their greater prevalence, and the spirit of candour which one hopes will spread with the progress of the world, will lead to their recognition, if only as an inevitable evil. The first step in the direction of such candour must be taken by the general admission of normal but illicit relations, and the facilitation of divorce, or possibly even the reconstruction of the system of marriage. Such advance must necessarily come from the more educated and liberal classes. Since 'unnatural' means 'removed from nature', only the most civilized, because the least natural, class of society can be expected to tolerate such a product of civilization.

I advance, therefore, the perfectly accepted theory that cases of dual personality do exist, in which the feminine and the masculine elements alternately preponderate. I advance this in an impersonal and scientific spirit, and claim that I am qualified to speak with the intimacy a professional scientist could acquire only after years of study and indirect information, because I have the object of study always to hand, in my own heart, and can gauge the exact truthfulness of what my own experience tells me. However frank, people would always keep back something. I can't keep back anything from myself.

I think Violet stayed on for about five days after that. All the time I was in fantastic spirits; and, not realizing how different she was from me in many ways, I made her follow me on wild courses all over the country, and, because she knew she had me only lightly hooked, she obeyed without remonstrance. There was very little between us during those days, only an immense excitement and a growing wish to go away somewhere alone together. This wish was carried out, by arranging to go down to Cornwall for the inside of a week; it was the first time I had ever been away from Harold, and he obviously minded my going.

She no longer flirted, and got rid of the last person she had been engaged to, when we went to Cornwall. But there was a man out in France, who used to write to her; she hardly knew him, and I wasn't jealous. He was called Denys Trefusis. She described him to me as fiery – hair like gold wire, blue eyes starting out of his head, and winged nostrils. I listened, not very much interested. I now hate him more than I have ever hated anyone in this life, or am likely to; and there is no injury I would not do him with the utmost pleasure.

Well, the whole of that summer she was mine – a mad and irresponsible summer of moonlight nights, and infinite escapades, and passionate letters, and music, and poetry. Things were not tragic for us then, because although we cared passionately we didn't care deeply – not like now, though it was deepening all the time; no, things weren't tragic, they were rapturous and new, and one side of my life was opened to me, and, to hide nothing, I found things out about my own temperament that I had never been sure of before. Of course I wish now that I had never made those discoveries. One doesn't miss what one doesn't know, and now life is made wretched for me by privations. I often long for ignorance and innocence. I think that if anything happened to bring my friendship with Violet to an end, I might have the strength of mind to blot all that entirely out of my life.

Paris . . . We were there for about a week, living in a flat that was lent us in the Palais Royal. Even now the intoxication of some of those hours in Paris makes me see confusedly; other hours were, I admit, wretched, because Denys came (the war being just over), and I wanted Violet to myself. But the evenings were ours. I have never told a soul of what I did. I hesitate to write it here, but I must; shirking the truth here would be like cheating oneself playing patience. I dressed as a boy. It was easy, because I could put a khaki bandage round my head, which in those days was so common that it attracted no attention at all. I browned my face and hands. It must have been successful, because no one looked at me at all curiously or suspiciously – never once, out of the many times I did it. My height of course was my great advantage. I looked like a rather untidy young man, a sort of undergraduate, of about nineteen. It was marvellous fun, all the more so because there was always the risk of being found out. Of course it was easy in the Palais Royal because I could let myself in and out by a latchkey; in hotels it was more difficult. I had done it once already in England; that was one of the boldest things I ever did. I will tell about it: I changed in my own house in London late one evening (the darkened streets made me bold), and drove with Violet in a taxi as far as Hyde Park Corner. There I got out. I never felt so free as when I stepped off the kerb, down Piccadilly, alone, and knowing that if I met my own mother face to face she would take no notice of me. I walked along, smoking a cigarette, buying a newspaper off a little boy who called me 'sir', and being accosted now and then by women. In this way I strolled from Hyde Park Corner to Bond Street, where I met Violet and took her in a taxi to Charing Cross. (The extraordinary thing was, how natural it all was for me). Nobody, even in the glare of the station, glanced at me twice. I had wondered about my voice, but found I could sink it sufficiently. Well, I took Violet as far as Orpington by train, and there we found a lodging house where we could get a room. The landlady was very benevolent and I said Violet was my wife. Next day of course I had to put on the same clothes, although I was a little anxious about the daylight, but again nobody took the slightest notice. We went to Knole!, which was, I think, brave. Here I slipped into the stables, and emerged as myself.

Well, this discovery was too good to be wasted, and in Paris I practically lived in that role. Violet used to call me Julian. We dined together every evening in cafés and restaurants, and went to all the theatres. I shall never forget the evenings when we walked back slowly to our flat through the streets of Paris. I, personally, had never felt so free in my life. Perhaps we have never been so happy since. When we got back to the flat, the windows all used to be open onto the courtyard of the Palais Royal, and the fountains splashed below. It was all incredible – like a fairty-tale.

22   It couldn't go on for ever, and at the end of the week we

left for Monte Carlo, stopping on the way at St Raphael. The weather was perfect, Monte Carlo was perfect, Violet was perfect. Again as Julian, I took her to a dance there, and had a success with a French family, who asked me to come and play bridge with them, and, I think, had an eye on me for their daughter, a plain girl whose head I tried to turn with compliments. They said '*On voit que monsieur est valseur*', and their son, a French officer, asked me about my '*blessure*', and we exchanged war reminiscences.

I didn't go back at Christmas. I didn't go back till nearly the end of March, and everybody was very angry with me, and I felt like suicide after those four wild and radiant months. The whole of that time is dreadful, a nightmare. Harold was in Paris, and I was alone with Mother and Dada, who were both very angry, and wanted me to give Violet up. (There had been a lot of scandal, by then.) On the other hand, Denys had been in England a month, and was agitating to announce his engagement to Violet. Violet was like a hunted creature. I could have prevented the engagement by very few words, but I thought that would be too outrageously selfish; there was Violet's mother, a demon of a woman, longing to get her safely married, and having told all London that she was going to marry Denys. She had already so bad a reputation for breaking engagements that this would have been the last straw. Besides, we both thought she would gain more liberty by marrying, and Denys was prepared to marry her on her own terms – that is, of merely brotherly relations.

I was absolutely miserable. I went to Brighton, alone, in a great empty dust-sheeted house, and all night I used to lie awake, and all day I used to wonder whether I wouldn't throw myself over the cliffs. Everyone questioned me as to why I looked so ill. On the fifth day Violet's engagement was announced in the papers; I bought the paper at Brighton station and nearly fainted as I read it, although I had expected to find it there. Not very long after that I went to Paris, to join Harold, who by that time knew the whole truth of the affair. I was terribly unhappy in Paris. When I came back to London, Violet began to declare that nothing would induce her to go through with the thing, and that I must save her from it by taking her away; in fact I believe she used Denys very largely as a lever to get me to do so. Living permanently with me had become an obsession in her mind. I don't absolutely remember the process in detail, but I know that I ended by consenting. After that we were both less unhappy; I could afford to see her ostensibly engaged to Denys when I knew that instead of marrying him she was coming away with me. I really intended to take her; we had every plan made. We were to go the day before her wedding – not sooner, because we thought we should be overtaken and brought back. It was of course only this looking-forward which enabled me to endure the period of her engagement.

Then about five days before her wedding I suddenly got by the same post three miserable letters from Harold, who had scented danger, because, in order to break it to him more or less gently (and also because I was in a dreadful state of mind myself during all that time), I had been writing him letters full of hints. When I read those letters something snapped in my mind. I saw Harold, all sweet and gentle and dependent upon me. Violet was there. She was terrified. I remember saying, 'It's no good, I can't take you away.' She implored me by everything she could think of, but I was obdurate. We went up to London together, Violet nearly off her head, and me repeating to myself phrases out of Harold's letters to give me strength. I telegraphed to him to say I was coming to Paris; I had only one idea, to fly as quickly as I could and to put distance between me and temptation. I saw Violet twice more; once in my own house in London; she looked ill and changed; and once in the early morning at her mother's house, where I went to say goodbye to her on my way to the station. There was a dreary slut scrubbing the doorstep, for it was very early, and I stepped in over the soapy pail, and saw Violet in the morning-room. Then I went to Paris, alone. That is one of the worst days I remember. While I was in the train going to Folkestone I still felt I could change my mind and go back if I wanted to, for she had told me she would wait for me up to the very last minute, and would come straight away if I appeared, or telephoned for her. At Folkestone I felt it becoming more irrevocable, and tried to get off the boat again, but they were moving the gangway and pushed me back. I had Harold's letters with me, and kept reading them until they almost lost all sense. The journey had never seemed so slow; it remains with me simply as a nightmare. I couldn't eat, and tears kept running down my face. Harold met me at the Gare du Nord. I said I wanted to go straight back, but he said, 'No, no', and took me out to Versailles in a motor. The next day was Sunday, and he stayed with me all day. By then I had got such a reaction that I was feverishly cheerful, and he might have thought nothing was the matter. I gave him the book I was writing [*Challenge*], because I knew Violet would hate me to do that, as it was all about her. I was awake nearly all that night. Next day was Monday, 16 June [1919]; Harold had to go into Paris, and I sat quite dazed in my room holding my watch in my hand and watching the hands tick past the hour of Violet's wedding. All that time, I knew, she was expecting a pre-arranged message from me, which I never sent.

I was so stunned by all this at the time that I could not even think; it is only since then that I have realized how every minute has burnt itself into me.

On Tuesday night Violet and Denys came to Paris. On Wednesday I went to see her, at the Ritz. She was wearing clothes I had never seen before, but no wedding ring. I can't describe how terrible it all was – that meeting, and everything. It makes me physically ill to write about it and think about it, and my cheeks are burning. It was dreadful, dreadful. By then I had left Versailles, and was living alone in a small hotel. I took her there, I treated her savagely, I made love to her, I had her, I didn't care, I only wanted to hurt Denys, even though he didn't know of it. I make no excuse, except that I had suffered too much during the past week and was really scarcely responsible. The next day I saw Denys at an awful interview. Violet told him she had meant to run away with me instead of marrying him; she told him she didn't care for him. He got very white, and I thought he was going to faint. I restrained myself from saying much more. I wanted to say, 'Don't you know, you stupid fool, that she is mine in every sense of the word?', but I was afraid that he would kill her if I did that. That night I dined at the Ritz, and from the open window of her room Violet watched me, and Denys sobbed in the room behind her. That day seems to have made a great impression upon him, as he constantly referred to it in his letters to her afterwards.

After that they went away to St Jean de Luz, and I went to Switzerland with Harold, and then back to England alone. After three weeks Violet came back. Things were not quite so bad then. She had a house in Sussex, and Denys only came there for the weekends, and I spent all the rest of the week there. On the whole, however, she was on friendly terms with him, and I am bound to say that he was friendly as an angel to her, and above all he kept the promises he had made, which I think few men would have done. I think on the whole that that was the period when Violet liked him best.

It was not till the end of August that I agreed to go away

with Violet. Harold was still in Paris, and I could leave Ben and Nigel at Knole, so it was comparatively easy.

We didn't stay very long in Paris, but went on to Monte Carlo en route for Greece. A complication arose over Denys announcing his arrival at Cannes. Violet didn't want to go; she wanted to make off, but I thought that if he arrived at Cannes confidently expecting her and then found she had bolted, he might do anything in a fit of despair. So I took her to Cannes, and went on myself to Paris; she was to tell Denys and I Harold, we hated leaving one another, even for (as we thought) a few days. We had been together two months. But when I got to Paris I found Harold with an abscess in the knee, and he had to be operated, and had a great deal of pain, so of course I dismissed every idea of letting him know anything was amiss. I stayed with him a fortnight (Mother was there too), and then went to England to see after Ben and Nigel. Violet came back to England a day or two later, and Harold was to follow. In the meantime, Violet, Denys and I met at a grotesque interview in London, when he asked me how much money I should have to keep Violet and myself on if we went away, so that I felt like a young man wanting to marry Violet and being interviewed by her father. Denys, who had come to see me by his own request, was very quiet and business-like, and looked like death. We did not shake hands. He turned to Violet and asked her if she wished to renounce everything and live with me. She was frightened, and asked for a week. We both agreed to that, and to abide by her decision, and he went away.

On the day that Harold came home Violet tried to rush things. She telephoned to me and told me Denys had said we must be gone by the following evening or not at all. Like a fool I believed her. This entailed telling Harold the moment he arrived. I met him at Victoria; he was very lame and on two sticks; the recollection of him goes through me like a stab even now. We dined at his parents' house, and after dinner I went upstairs to his room and told him I was leaving England with Violet next day. He broke down and cried. Then his mother came in, and I told her what I was going to do, and why; and of course she implored me not to; she had taken off her false hair, and although she didn't realize it a bit, was one of the most pathetic and sincere figures at that moment I have ever beheld. I felt so alien from the whole kindly, law-abiding house; I felt like a pariah, and his mother's tolerance only increased my shame; she didn't push me away, but put both her arms round me and said that nothing I could do was wrong but only mistaken. I felt blackened, and I was so unhappy, and felt my alienation from them and my affinity with Violet so keenly that I only wanted to fly where I would not pollute their purity any longer.

Next day I called for her in a taxi in London, and we left for Lincoln.

It was bitterly cold, but we were happy in Lincoln. I took her with me to the fen country, which I was writing a book 29 about; that was the object of going to Lincoln. Then we came back to London to the Liverpool Street hotel, and she telephoned for Denys, who came, and she told him she was leaving England next day. I was not present, but I saw him. As we were waiting for a taxi with our luggage in the hall of the hotel next morning, he came in again. He asked her to go and speak to him, but I don't know what he said. He gave her a long letter he had written her, and she gave it to me to read in the taxi on the way to Victoria, and having read it I did the only thing I am in the very least proud of: I said I would give her up if she would go back to him. She refused vehemently and said nothing would induce her to, not even my leaving her. I urged her – I really did urge her; he had written her a letter that really touched me. I travelled down to Dover with her, and all the way I tried to persuade her. But she was adamant. The only concession she would make was to start for France by herself, because she seemed to think he would mind that less. So I saw her off, absolutely firm in her resolution, but childishly terrified of the journey on the boat, and I was to join her at Amiens the next day.

I remained alone at Dover, watching her boat out of sight, and then I went to a lodging house and got myself a room for the night. I lunched, and feeling very disconsolate I walked down to the station and stood staring out over the sea, when turning round I saw Denys coming towards me. He looked very anxious, and wore big motor gloves. He said, 'Where's Violet?', and I answered that she had gone. He wanted to follow her. I took him back to my lodging house, and he paced up and down my bedroom there for the rest of the afternoon. At first I would not tell him where she had gone, but as he threatened to stay with me until I left Dover, saying that he knew I was going to join her, I told him I was leaving next day. He promised not to steal a march on me, and we said we would go together and give her the choice between us. I did not hate him in the least then; I was only very sorry. We stalked out together to the post office, and sent telegrams to Violet's family and to mine, and then parted with extreme grimness. During the evening I got a panic-stricken telegram from Violet, which I telephoned through to Denys.

It poured with rain, and the wind seemed stronger than ever; I went out, and was blown clean across the road. The sea was mud-coloured, and very rough; even the ships in the harbour rocked violently, and outside the harbour the waves flung showers of spray over the piers. I never remember such a gale. I went to the boat to get a cabin, and there encountered Denys on the same errand. The sight of us both bribing for cabins in the purser's office was so comic that it made us less grim to one another. I don't know what Denys thought, but personally I was rather exhilarated at the prospect of steaming out into that storm and insecurity after the nervous and inactive hours I had lived through.

Anyhow, that symbolic crossing beat cordiality into Denys and into me, and we joked about sea-sick remedies, and he dared me to smoke, and by the time we drew alongside at Calais he was asking me to lunch with him in the buffet. He then said he would look after my luggage if I would go on and get a table. I went into the buffet, and there Violet rushed up to me, white and shaking and nearly hysterical. I said, 'Good God, why aren't you at Amiens? Denys is with me', and she said we must get away at once, but at that moment he came in. We realized at once that she was ill and starving (she had had nothing to eat since twenty-four hours or more), so we made her sit down and eat chicken and drink champagne. She said she had left all her possessions at Amiens, but there was no question of taking her there that day, or of anything except putting her to bed and getting a doctor. We all three trundled across Calais in a shut-cab, found a hotel, and started putting her to bed; but it was so dirty that we took her to another one. She was completely docile in our hands, and we were too busy getting her hot-water bottles, sponges, soup, and a doctor, to realize the absurdity of the whole thing. What made it more ridiculous, was that Denys and I were given communicating rooms, while she was a little way off. When we had got her safely to bed, we both sat in her room and beamed at her with relief. She had recovered then, and amused us by telling us stories of her adventures on the way to Amiens. We had both been anxious about her, and were conscious of nothing but delight in merely having her safe; at least I know that was what I felt, and I am sure from Denys's manner that he felt the same. The immense problem that the three of us had got to solve, and all the agony and heartburning its solution must entail for one of us – all that was set aside by triple consent. We were all gay, we were even light-hearted, not negatively, but positively; it was as though time were suspended, and all human relations suspended too, except Denys's and my common love for Violet. We had no hostility, I think, towards one another. We were foes who, while our enmity was in abeyance, were prepared to love one another. Our enmity was an extrinsic, not an intrinsic thing. We argued and discussed upon all the detached topics that were as dear to Denys as they were to me; we discussed music, poetry and immortality, and all the while Violet lay like a princess propped up by a pillow in an enormous bed and listened to us with a *narquois* expression of amazed amusement, and frank relish at the farcical turn affairs had taken. This was after dinner. We had all three dined in her bedroom, and Denys and I had, in turn, waited upon her. She was altogether charming and amusing that evening. At the beginning of dinner our lips were twitching with the temptation to *fou rire*, and Violet alone saved the situation. After dinner, as I have said, it was Denys and I who talked. I saw that evening how intelligent he was, how absorbed in un-sordid things; I even saw with regret what good friends we might have been under other circumstances; and above all I was touched by his very naive joy at having Violet safe, and present; I was touched by this, because I shared and could understand it.

Next morning Violet was better, and we three break-fasted together, and afterwards got a motor to go across to Boulogne. Still the essential subject had not been raised, except as a joke on the previous evening by Denys, who suggested that we should go to Jamaica and grow sugar. We were both grimmer again, realizing that the discussion could not much longer be put off. The motor drive was a dreary business. It was a black day, and the road lay across bleak country, hedgeless, monotonous country, and once we nearly got smashed up, and Denys said to me, 'Perhaps that would be the best solution after all.' We lunched at Boulogne, then took the train to Amiens. We had agreed to discuss it at Amiens, but in the train in the midst of writing limericks and jokes, Denys wrote on a piece of paper that he knew Violet's mind was made up, and that he would leave us at Amiens and go on himself to Paris, never to see Violet again. Everything was tragic again in an instant. I was tongue-tied, and could say nothing. We were then about two hours distant from Amiens, and feeling that the journey would really be too painful, I went away and sat in the compartment next door. Denys cried the whole way to Amiens, and at Amiens Violet and I got out, and so did he, as he had to get into another train; he looked awful as he went away, and Violet and I were alone.

That was a bad two hours.

We went to the Hôtel du Rhin, where Violet's things already were. I think I was more sorry for Denys than she
was. If he had not made up his mind like that in the train I

had meant to urge her again to go with him, although I knew it would be quite useless. I could not understand her indifference towards him, for even I was oppressed by the thought of what he must be suffering, and of what he would suffer next day on his way through from Paris to London, when he passed through Amiens knowing that Violet was still there with me. I was so much disturbed by all this, that I telephoned myself to Paris to find out if he was all right, and was told that he had already left for London.

We spent that day looking at the devastations of Amiens and at the very lovely cathedral. I telegraphed to Harold where I was in case he should be anxious. (I did not know that he had had no letters or telegrams from me at all, as he was by then looking for me in England, having crossed in the same gale, only in the opposite direction.) Violet and I meant to motor past Paris (I couldn't bear to go actually into Paris where I thought Harold was) and then to get a train and go to Sicily. If she had been well we should probably have done this the same day, but she was still ill from the effects of her fright and starvation, so we stayed in Amiens. After dinner that night her father [Colonel George Keppel] arrived at our hotel. He was pompous, theatrical, and unimpressive. He stormed at us, and it was all we could do to keep from laughing. The tiresome part was, that he had wired for Denys, and refused to leave us lest we should slip away.

Now comes the worst part. Denys and Harold arrived

together by aeroplane early in the morning. I was very much astonished, because of course I had thought Harold was in Paris all this time, getting letters more or less all the time from me. He came up to my room, hard on Violet's heels, and told me to pack. Then there was an unpleasant scene. I sat on the window-sill, and Violet stood near me, and we defied first Harold and then Denys, and then both together. This sounds absurd and childish, and so I dare say it was. Denys was the most silent of all; he just looked at Violet while she abused him. The upshot of it was that we refused to leave each other, and Harold said we should be starved out by having someone always with us till we gave way – it was all undignified and noisy to a degree, and I hated it, and was rude to Harold, and he said a lot of silly things that showed him in a wrong light to Violet, and I was sorry about that too. Then Violet and I went together and met Denys in a passage, and he leaned against the wall looking like a stained-glass window saint, very pale and frail, and quite golden-haired, while she said she loathed him, and never to my dying day shall I forget the look on his face. He said nothing at all, but again only stared at her, and if he had slipped down and died at our feet I should scarcely have been surprised.

Then I went upstairs again, to where Harold was sitting in my room, and he tried to talk to me sensibly, and I was less rude, but firm. Then he said a thing which made all the room spin round my head. He said, 'Are you sure Violet is as faithful to you as she makes you believe? Because Denys has told your mother quite a different story.' I thought I should go mad when he said that. I rushed downstairs, and at the foot of the stairs I met Denys. I stopped him and said, 'I am very sorry, but I must ask you the most terribly indiscreet question: have you ever been really married to Violet?' He answered, 'I refuse to tell you; that is a matter which lies entirely between Violet and myself.' (I can remember every single one of the words we all spoke at that time.) I caught his sleeve; I kept him; I insisted. I said, 'If you tell me you have, I swear to you I will never set eyes on Violet again.' He hesitated a little at that, and then said again, 'I can't answer.'

I let him go; I went into the restaurant where Violet was sitting at a little table waiting for her breakfast. I went straight up to her and said (as though the words were being put into my lips), 'Why have you not told me you have deceived me with Denys?' I never saw such absolute terror leap into anyone's face. She stammered something, I don't know what. I said, 'You have belonged to him.' She said 'Yes.' I said 'When?', and she said, 'The night before we went to Lincoln.' Yet I knew she was a virgin.

I don't know what I said then; I only know that I broke away from her as she tried to hold me, and said quite wildly that I was going away from her. She followed me, and we got into the sitting-room; somehow the doors and woodwork of the sitting-room were pocked with bullet marks. Denys was there too, and she kept saying all kinds of wild things, like, 'Let me explain', or, 'Tell her it isn't true', and I kept saying only that I wanted to go. I was half mad with pain and not understanding. She was crying, and held me so strongly that I couldn't get away till Denys helped me. Then I rushed upstairs while he held her in the sitting-room, and I packed my things, blind with passion and pain, not able to think or speak, but only thinking that I must get away at all costs. I went downstairs, and found that Harold was with her. Denys was guarding the door. I had just enough sense left to beg him not to leave her for a moment. When Harold came out I went in, although they tried to prevent me. I kissed Violet. Then I went away as quickly as I could, in a motor, with Harold. We had to get his bag out of the aeroplane, and we waited a long time on the aerodrome. That was awful, as Amiens was so near, and we had to drive through Amiens again to get to the station, but I heard Harold tell the chauffeur to avoid the street where the hotel was, and we went by slums. There was no train for Paris for about an hour.

Harold had lunch in the buffet, but I couldn't eat anything. I saw Violet's father also going to Paris by the same train, so I knew she was alone with Denys, and I hated him then as I never had before. But I couldn't think of anything clearly at all. Harold took me to his hotel in Paris; I didn't care where I went or what became of me. I couldn't cry. I don't remember when we got to Paris, or what I did until it was time for dinner. I had not swallowed a mouthful of food all day, and I was beginning to feel slightly light-headed, so I went down to the restaurant and had some soup. I began to get the usual reaction after one had gone through too much strain, and in consequence I started talking to Harold and making jokes, and all the time a hammer in my head went 'Violet! Violet!', and it was rather like the day before her wedding, when I was at Versailles with Harold.

We hadn't been in the restaurant long when I saw Violet come in. I dropped my knife and fork, and went to her; it was like warmth rushing back when one has been deadly cold, because for the first second I forgot that something much worse than mere distance had parted us. Harold told me to take her upstairs, and I was shut into the sitting-room alone with her. I got behind a chair so that she shouldn't come near me; I was shivering all over. I don't remember our conversation very distinctly; I remember saying over and over again, 'You mustn't ask me to think; I've been stunned and I haven't recovered.' She was very urgent and desperate, and said that if I cast her off altogether she would throw herself into the river, and I am sure this was true. She also said that things had not been quite as I had first believed. She had never belonged to Denys, although matters had gone halfway in that direction. I still kept shivering and saying that I couldn't think. At that moment Harold and Denys came in. She asked Harold to go out, and asked Denys to corroborate what she had just told me. He walked up and down the room and seemed to be struggling with himself. Then he said, 'This must never go further than this room; I promise you that there has never been anything of that kind between Violet and me.' I could have cried with relief, but still it was bad enough that she should have deceived me even to a certain extent – especially on the very night when I was innocently making every disposition to give up everything in the world for her next day. That was what hurt me most bitterly. When I was again alone with her I said I could not bear to see her for at least two months.

Next day she left Paris for the South of France, and every day she used to telephone to me from the various provincial towns where they stopped for the night; and every day her voice was fainter as the distances increased. It must have been a nightmare journey – Denys collapsed and fell ill, but she urged on the motor as though she had been driven by a demon, and it was on that journey, I think, that Denys finally lost what slight hope he still had that she might come to care for him.

I won't say what I went through during the six weeks that passed before I saw her again. I seemed to know every variety of torment – that of longing and aching miserably for someone in whom I had lost faith, that of loving to desperation someone in whose worth I no longer believed. Before, I had always buoyed myself with the thought that although she might hold no other moral precept, at least she was whole-hearted and true where she did love. To this day I don't understand what prompted her to give in, even so little. I think it was a mixture of pity and remorse because she knew she was intending to leave him for good the next day, and she had certainly told me for weeks that he was increasingly importunate. Anyhow I don't want to speculate, it's too painful.

I stayed in Paris for some time, then came back to England. Violet was at Bordighera, living in a villa, while he lived in an hotel. In March I went out to join her at Avignon. I hadn't seen her for six weeks, and I travelled straight through. It ought to have been a good meeting, but it wasn't. Three hours after my arrival we were already quarrelling because she had apparently thought she could persuade me to stay with her for good, and was angry when she found she couldn't. We motored from Avignon to Bordighera, and quarrelled the whole time, and I was acutely wretched. Then at San Remo I lost my head and said I would stay, and for a few days we were happy. We went on to Venice, but I don't really look back on that journey with much pleasure. She was ill, with a touch of jaundice, a most unromantic complaint, and I could do nothing with her, especially after I had gone back on what I had said at San Remo. I admit that I behaved badly over that. One ought not to allow oneself the luxury of losing one's head.

She wanted to remain abroad by herself, but I couldn't allow that – she is as helpless as a child, and would happily have entrusted her passport, her ticket, her jewels, and her money to the first person who offered to relieve her of the responsibility of looking after them, and anyway I saw the sort of life she would lead, ranging from hotel to hotel, quite irresponsible, and horribly lonely, so I dragged her reluctant person back to England with me.

Those were very cruel weeks, when our only preoccupation seemed to be the desire to score off one another, or to catch one another out. The Amiens incident had (not unnaturally) destroyed all trust on my part, and the temporary death of the possibility of our living together drove her into the usual embittering despair. She tried again to get me to go away, by making me believe that Denys threatened to break his promises to her; but I was more wary now, and before making any promise I made her write to Denys, a letter whose reply showed quite clearly that he had not attempted to break his promises nor had any intention of doing so.

There was a strange period when Denys went away by himself to Devonshire, and wrote her daily letters from there telling her that he no longer cared for her. In fact when he returned to London he refused for a long time to set eyes on her, and she spent that time with me, chiefly at Hindhead (Harold was in Paris), but of course when Denys saw her, everything began again. He cared for her too fatally for it to die like that. There was one evening when she was staying with me, and he telephoned to her to come at once; it was after dinner; I got out my car and drove her to the station, but the last train had gone, so I drove her on to London, to the hotel where Denys was waiting for her, and went myself to lodgings I knew of, where I had to have the room of someone who was away; I had nothing whatever with me, and it took me ages to find anywhere to sleep. Of course I dared not go to Mother's house, as it was after midnight.

The whole summer was made up of episodes like that. We weren't happy – how could we be? We were happy once for five days when we went motoring; we went from Hindhead to Rye, and it was a great success, but it didn't make up for all the wretchedness and jealousy and turmoil we went through at other times. Other people were wretched too; I mean, Denys, who actually fell into consumption, and had to go and do a cure in Holland, where Violet's mother had a house, and Violet of course had to go too, for five weeks. During the whole of those five weeks we didn't quarrel by letter, and when she came back it was like two flames leaping together. She arrived from Holland at one station, and drove straight across London to another station where I was waiting for her, and we went down to her house in the country where we spent four absolutely unclouded days.

I am writing now in the light of later events, and writing in the midst of great unhappiness which I try to conceal from poor Harold, who is an angel upon earth. It is possible that I may never see Violet again, or that I may see her once again before we are parted, or that we may meet in future years as strangers; it is also possible that she may not choose to live; in any case it has come about indirectly owing to me, while I remain safe, secure and undamaged save in my heart. The injustice and misfortune of the whole thing oppresses me hourly; it gives me an awful sense of doom – Violet's doom, which she herself has consistently predicted.

Afterword by Nigel Nicolson

Vita's elopement with Violet Trefusis was the only crisis of her marriage. Having survived it, she and Harold were able to confront with equanimity many later incidents so menacing that each separately would have broken up most homes. After Amiens there was six foot of water under their keel, and their rowboat, which had nearly foundered on the rocks, slid easily away from the shoals which it touched offshore. Violet had shown them that nothing could destroy their love, which was actually enhanced by the complete freedom they allowed each other. Both were completely frank about it, in speech and letters. It no longer required argument: simply a statement of fact and current emotion. Harold would refer to Vita's affairs as 'your muddles'; she to his as 'your fun'. No jealousy ever arose because of them. On his side there was only a concern that she might break the heart of someone else, a rival or the woman's husband, while she was more amused than worried by what was happening to him, knowing that he had these things under greater control. To scandal, or, in his case, to the law, they seem never to have given a thought, for their intellectual friends were infinitely tolerant, and they did not mind what was said by outsiders.

> I suppose [wrote Vita], that ninety-nine people out of a hundred, if they knew all about us, would call us wicked and degenerate. And yet I know with absolute certainty that there are not ninety-nine people out of a hundred less wicked and degenerate than we are. I don't want to boast, but we *are* alive, aren't we? And our two lives, outside and inside, are rich lives – not little meagre repetitions of meagre cerebral habits.

So carefree were they that quite often at Long Barn Harold's friend and Vita's would join the same weekend party, and the four of them would refer to the situation quite openly. Lady Sackville gives in her diary this instance of their attitude, her embarrassment leading her to an unfortunate choice of phrase:

> *23 Sept. 1923.* Vita is absolutely devoted to Harold, but there is nothing whatever sexual between them, which is strange in such a young and good-looking couple. She is not in the least jealous of him, and willingly allows him to relieve himself with anyone. They both openly said so when I was staying at Long Barn, and Reggie Cooper [who had been at Wellington and Constantinople with Harold] was there too. It shocked me extremely . . .

To this easy relationship they gave a moral base, both having analytical minds, and they evolved a 'formula' for their marriage, 'a firm, elastic formula', said Harold, 'which makes it so easy for us both to duplicate the joys of love and life, and to halve their miseries'; or, as she put it to him, 'We are sure of each other, in this odd, strange, detached, intimate, mystical relationship which we could never explain to any outside person.' The formula ran something like this: what mattered most was that each should trust the other absolutely. 'Trust', in most marriages, means fidelity. In theirs it meant that they would always tell each other of their infidelities, give warning of approaching emotional crises and, whatever happened, return to their common centre in the end. Vita once put her 'little creed' for Harold in these words: 'To love me whatever I do. To believe my motives are not mean. Not to credit tales without hearing my own version. To give up everything and everybody for me in the last resort.'

The basis of their marriage was mutual respect, enduring love and 'a common sense of values'. There were certain things which were wrong absolutely, and so long as they agreed on what those things were, it did not matter much if in other ways they behaved differently or even (in the eyes of the world) outrageously. When we were children, they divided misdemeanours into 'crimes' and 'sins', and applied the same rule to themselves. Crimes were naughtinesses, for which we were punished. (My mother was not very good at that. When I broke the greenhouse windows, she decided to spank me on the bottom with her hairbrush, but never having done such a 47 thing before, she used the brush bristle side downwards, and the bristles were very soft.) Sins were so dreadful that for them we were never punished at all: their very exposure was enough. There were only three sins: cruelty, dishonesty and indolence. Vita herself had been guilty of the first in 1919–20; never again. Harold was innocent of them all. Their morality can be summed up as consideration for other people, particularly for each other, and the development of their natural talents to the full. It was an amalgam of the Christian virtues and the eighteenth-century concept of the civilized life.

In 1929 they debated on BBC radio their ideas about marriage, and this was their conclusion:

Harold:	You agree that a successful marriage is the greatest of human benefits?
Vita:	Yes.
Harold:	And that it must be based on love guided by intelligence?
Vita:	Yes.
Harold:	That an essential condition is a common sense of values?
Vita:	Yes.
Harold:	That the only things that will stave off marital nerves are modesty, good humour and, above all, occupation?
Vita:	Yes.
Harold:	And give and take?

Vita:	And give and take.
Harold:	And mutual esteem. I do not believe in the permanence of any love which is based on pity, or the protective or maternal instincts. It must be based on respect.
Vita:	Yes, I agree. The caveman plus sweet-little-thing theory is long past. It was a theory insulting to the best qualities of both.

Marriage, they thought (but not for a BBC audience in 1929), was 'unnatural'. Marriage was only tolerable for people of strong character and independent minds if it were regarded as a lifetime association between intimate friends. It was a bond which should last only as long as both wanted it to. (Both, for this reason, were strongly in favour of easier divorce.) But as a happy marriage is 'the greatest of human benefits', husband and wife must strive hard for its success. Each must be subtle enough to mould their characters and behaviour to fit the other's, facet to facet, convex to concave. The husband must develop the feminine side of his nature, the wife her masculine side. He must cultivate the qualities of sympathy and intuition; she those of detachment, reason and decision. He must respond to tears; she must not miss trains.

As it happened, mutual adjustment was particularly easy for them, because they already possessed these qualities. Vita since her childhood had never ceased to regret that she was not born a boy. Once she quoted to Violet Queen

Elizabeth's magnificent phrase: 'Had I been crested not cloven, my Lords, you had not treated me thus.' She had inherited from her mother the aristocratic gift of command, and in most things was very competent. Harold had certain feminine attributes, his emotionalism and his clemency. Vita could be intimidating. Harold rarely was, though in social and diplomatic London he was a young lion. If they witnessed together an act of cruelty, such as a Greek peasant beating his donkey, he would express his horror; she would furiously intervene. He obeyed regulations with the instinct of a trained civil servant; she would protest, sometimes refuse. Harold had a sentimental side to his nature which she did not. He could be moved to tears by a film or play in which virtue was triumphant or innocence abused; she took both in her stride. She was the calculated-risk-taker in their marriage, sometimes to the peril of them both. The risks which he took were more spontaneous, motivated by a sudden surge of emotion, personal or political. But because they knew each other so intimately, and loved each other so deeply, neither was in the least irritated by these opposites. Vita would sometimes reproach him for being too mild, 'put upon' she said (for instance by the low fees he accepted from editors), and he would tease her about the odd gaps in her knowledge of the world, like her total inability to understand an Income Tax form or add up a simple column of figures, or her ineradicable belief that rivers like the Nile which flow northwards must run uphill. Never, never did I see them lose their tempers with each other, and my mother told me that it happened only once. The incident was typical. She came into his room one evening and he shouted, 'Go away!' Hurt and angry, she flung at him the lilies which she was carrying, and slammed the door. He rushed after her to explain that his birthday-present – a bust of Hermes – which he was to give her as a surprise the next morning was sitting unwrapped on his table.

No reader could fail to be convinced of their love for each other if I were to give constant quotations from their letters spread over fifty years, but such an anthology would become tedious and cloying in the mass. In most marriages love after a time becomes inarticulate, or is expressed in bed. In their marriage there was no bed, but both, being writers, found infinite pleasure in analyzing their emotions. As they were so often apart, they wrote to each other thousands of letters, and these formed the warp and woof of their marriage, which was thus continuously enriched and rewoven. She spoke of 'the great triumph of being loved by you', and both were perpetually amazed at their good fortune. Each loved most in the other the qualities which she or he did not possess, Vita his leniency, Harold her wildfire romanticism, and it amused them to identify the differences between them in order to highlight the qualities they shared. They had many common interests: literature and travel and gardening; their children; their cottages; their possessions; their tastes; their plans, past and present; memories of joy and near-disaster. All these things formed a rich *pot-pourri* which never staled. Separation sharpened its tang. Painful as it was, absence often seemed to them like an illusion: the other might be in the next room. 'Your letter', he once wrote to her from Persia, 'makes me feel that distance does not matter, and that loneliness is only a physical, not a spiritual, displacement.' They could reach out over continents to feel the other's pulse and measure it exactly. They could be together at Long Barn for hours, reading in silence, and then both speak suddenly at the same moment. This communion of feeling was as expressive as a touch or glance. If one were ill or in imagined danger (and to Vita every taxi seemed like a threat to him, every aeroplane certain murder), they would undergo tortures of anxiety. Harold would cable across half the world for the latest news of her mild attack of sciatica. A hostile paragraph about him in a newspaper would drive her to despair, while he would worry agonizingly about one of her lectures or broadcasts which alarmed her. It was their constant involvement in each other's lives and feelings, caring without interfering, which was both the expression of their love and its strength. In the middle of the Second War, Vita wrote for Harold a poem which was read by the Poet Laureate, Cecil Day-Lewis, at their joint memorial service in 1968:

I must not tell how dear you are to me.
It is unknown, a secret from myself
Who should know best. I would not if I could
Expose the meaning of such mystery.

I loved you then, when love was Spring, and May.
Eternity is here and now, I thought;
The pure and perfect moment briefly caught
As in your arms, but still a child, I lay.

Loved you when summer deepened into June
And those fair, wild, ideal dreams of youth
Were true yet dangerous and half unreal
As when Endymion kissed the mateless moon.

But now when autumn yellows all the leaves
And thirty seasons mellow our long love,
How rooted, how secure, how strong, how rich,
How full the barn that holds our garnered sheaves!

The centre of our lives during later boyhood and
adolescence was Sissinghurst Castle, near Cranbrook in
Kent, where both our parents lived for more than thirty
years and where both died. The garden is a portrait of their
marriage. Harold made the design, Vita did the planting.
In the firm perspectives of the vistas, the careful siting of an
urn or statue, the division of the garden by hedges and
walls and buildings into a series of separate gardens, the
calculated alternation between straight lines and curved,
one can trace his classical hand. In the overflowing
clematis, figs, vines and wistaria, in the rejection of violent
colour or anything too tame or orderly, one discovers her
romanticism. Wild flowers must be allowed to invade the
garden; if plants stray over a path, they must not be cut

back, the visitor must duck; rhododendrons must be banished in favour of their tenderer cousin, the azalea; roses must not electrify, but seduce; and when a season has produced its best, that part of the garden must be allowed to lie fallow for another year, since there is a cycle in nature which must not be disguised. It is eternally renewable, like a play with acts and scenes: there can be a change of cast, but the script remains the same. Permanence and mutation are the secrets of this garden.

Harold and Vita had long ago reconciled their different temperaments, and they created for themselves a life which suited both perfectly – separation during the week, reunion at weekends. She when alone would garden all day, and write half the night: he in London, first at King's Bench Walk in the Temple, and after the war at Albany, Piccadilly, was busy, social, industrious. He would carry up from Sissinghurst on Monday baskets of flowers, bring down on Friday the London news which still entertained her so long as she was not involved, and in between, every day, they wrote to each other, and each kept all the other's letters. Few marriages can be better documented. What cannot be preserved except in memory is the gentleness of their reunions. They did not 'leap together like two flames', as when Violet returned from Holland, but berthed like sister-ships. There was always a certain bustle, the business of unpacking and tea, the tour of the garden and the changing of clothes, but soon they settled down to their easy companionship, allowing words to trickle into the crevasses of the other's mind, feeding each other with impressions of what they had read or heard, stimulating, reassuring, teasing by turns – a process which was half solicitous, half provocative, always tender. It was the alternation of excitement and calm in their lives, the 'succession of privacies' as Harold described the charm of Sissinghurst itself, the sense that each was always available to the other though neither would intrude unasked, which made the later years of their marriage so consecrated and serene.

Vita died at Sissinghurst in June 1962, and Harold survived her by six years.

Phoenix 60p Paperbacks

History/Biograpy/Travel
The Empire of Rome A.D. 98–190 *Edward Gibbon*
The Prince *Machiavelli*
The Alan Clark Diaries: Thatcher's Fall *Alan Clark*
Churchill: Embattled Hero *Andrew Roberts*
The French Revolution *E.J. Hobsbawm*
Voyage Around the Horn *Joshua Slocum*
The Great Fire of London *Samuel Pepys*
Utopia *Thomas More*
The Holocaust *Paul Johnson*
Tolstoy and History *Isaiah Berlin*

Science and Philosophy
A Guide to Happiness *Epicurus*
Natural Selection *Charles Darwin*
Science, Mind & Cosmos *John Brockman, ed.*
Zarathustra *Friedrich Nietzsche*
God's Utility Function *Richard Dawkins*
Human Origins *Richard Leakey*
Sophie's World: The Greek Philosophers *Jostein Gaarder*
The Rights of Woman *Mary Wollstonecraft*
The Communist Manifesto *Karl Marx & Friedrich Engels*
Birds of Heaven *Ben Okri*

Fiction
Riot at Misri Mandi *Vikram Seth*
The Time Machine *H. G. Wells*
Love in the Night *F. Scott Fitzgerald*

The Murders in the Rue Morgue *Edgar Allan Poe*
The Necklace *Guy de Maupassant*
You Touched Me *D. H. Lawrence*
The Mabinogion *Anon*
Mowgli's Brothers *Rudyard Kipling*
Shancarrig *Maeve Binchy*
A Voyage to Lilliput *Jonathan Swift*

POETRY

Songs of Innocence and Experience *William Blake*
The Eve of Saint Agnes *John Keats*
High Waving Heather *The Brontes*
Sailing to Byzantium *W. B. Yeats*
I Sing the Body Electric *Walt Whitman*
The Ancient Mariner *Samuel Taylor Coleridge*
Intimations of Immortality *William Wordsworth*
Palgrave's Golden Treasury of Love Poems *Francis Palgrave*
Goblin Market *Christina Rossetti*
Fern Hill *Dylan Thomas*

LITERATURE OF PASSION

Don Juan *Lord Byron*
From Bed to Bed *Catullus*
Satyricon *Petronius*
Love Poems *John Donne*
Portrait of a Marriage *Nigel Nicolson*
The Ballad of Reading Gaol *Oscar Wilde*
Love Sonnets *William Shakespeare*
Fanny Hill *John Cleland*
The Sexual Labyrinth (for women) *Alina Reyes*
Close Encounters (for men) *Alina Reyes*